MISSION TRIP DEVOTIONS & JOURNAL

ANTICIPATE

Standard®
PUBLISHING
Bringing The Word to Life

Published by Standard Publishing, Cincinnati, Ohio
www.standardpub.com

Copyright © 2007 by CHRIST IN YOUTH

Project editor: Kelly Carr
Cover and interior design: The DesignWorks Group
Printed in: China

ISBN 978-0-7847-2189-6

13 12 11 10 09 08   9 8 7 6 5 4 3 2

READY?

Can you feel it right now—the anticipation building up inside? You're headed on a mission trip, so you'd better get ready!

No, I don't mean packing. You might be one of those personality types that has been packed for weeks (or at least you've made your packing list). Or maybe you wait until the night before to even think about what you're taking.

What I mean is getting ready in other ways—mentally, emotionally, spiritually. Whether it's your first mission trip or your fiftieth, whether you're headed to another country or down the street, you're going to face new challenges on this journey. And you'll want to be prepared.

- Who are the people your work will be impacting?

- What will the building projects, teaching time, and worship services be like?

- How will you get along with the other members of your team?

- What does God have in store for you to learn?

- How will God use you to make a difference?

These questions are just the beginning as you anticipate the importance of your trip.

ANTICIPATE

Anticipate. That word has been said several times now. In fact, it's the title of this book. And that's what your time of preparation is all about—anticipating the things God has for you to do for his kingdom on your upcoming mission trip.

This book has fifteen devotions and journaling space to help you prepare mentally, emotionally, and spiritually for your time of service. It will also help you anticipate the responsibility you have to share the love of Jesus through your actions and words.

These devotions were written by people who have served the Lord both in the U.S. and in places beyond. They share what God has taught them in order to help you listen for the Holy Spirit's guidance in your own preparation.

Anticipate what God is preparing you to do.

SOLID FOUNDATION

by Matt Gilchrist

One of my favorite summer activities growing up was our annual family vacation to the coast. In Oregon, the coast is not like what you would imagine on a typical beach. The weather is not nearly as warm, the water is frigid, and the waves are pretty lame—so people do not do much surfing or, for that matter, much of anything in the water. Instead of bodies tanning everywhere, the beach is known more for all the rocks and pieces of driftwood that are scattered across the sand. The Oregon coast is more of a peaceful place where you go for long walks to enjoy the scenery and the people you are with than it is a place packed with activity.

I remember the summer after my sixth grade school year during our annual pilgrimage to the coast. One evening, my parents and I took a long walk to enjoy the fresh air and beautiful scenery.

I was at the age where it was not cool to hang out with your parents, so I decided to run up ahead and pretend I was there on my own. I was hoping a beautiful young lady would see me and strike up a conversation. As I was running, I jumped off some of the various rocks along the beach and tried to launch myself high into the air. (Thinking about it now, I probably looked like a huge goober, definitely not the kind of guy my dream girl was looking for!) Off I went, running and leaping over and over again.

Due to the fun we were having, this particular walk took much longer than expected, and soon the lazy summer sun began to set behind the ocean. As it got darker, it became more difficult to see, but I pressed on.

SCREAMING LIKE A GIRL

As I continued my leaping adventure, I prepared myself for the greatest leap ever. Approaching the next rock, I coiled my legs as best I could, placed my foot square on the surface, and prepared to launch into orbit. Instead, the rock gave way, and I heard a horrible squishing and slurping sound. My leap never materialized. My legs collapsed, causing me to dive face-first into the sand in a complete wipeout.

I quickly gathered myself up, wiped the sand off my teeth, and turned around to see what had happened. I discovered it was not a rock I'd placed my foot on after all.

It was a dead seal!

My next response was classic, as I screamed liked a girl and ran back to where my parents were. I didn't leave their sides for the duration of the walk—or very often during the remainder of the vacation either.

I learned a valuable lesson that day: without a firm foundation, you cannot succeed. You have to start with a solid base, and from there you can launch yourself to new heights. Without a rock-solid foundation, we are all destined for a horrible wipeout.

BUILDING ON SOLID GROUND

If someone asked you what a solid, Christian foundation was made up of, what would you say?

In Matthew 7:24-27, Jesus closes his Sermon on the Mount with a challenge to his listeners about a strong foundation. He says that those who hear his words and put them into practice are like a wise man who builds on a solid foundation. He also says that people who hear his words and do not put them into practice are fools.

In my lifetime, I have met many people who have heard the right things and know what God wants, yet never live that way. For them it is enough to be in church and to know the right answers that make them look good in Sunday school class or satisfy their parents' questions. But their hearts never change. On the outside they may look and sound like Christians, but when you dig a little deeper, when a storm happens in their lives, or when they are pushed beyond their comfort zones, their houses crumble.

While growing up, I loved being in Sunday school and singing the song about this passage of Scripture. My favorite part was always when we got to the end of the verses and the house either stood firm or "went *crash!*" I think it was partially because we were allowed to be loud and crazy at those parts—but little did I know I was learning a valuable lesson about the Christian walk.

HEADING FOR A WIPEOUT

James reiterates Jesus' teaching: "Anyone, then, who knows the good he ought to do and doesn't do it, sins" (James 4:17). No longer is it good enough to simply know the right things—we have to do them. If we do not practice the lifestyle we are called to, we are sinning. If we simply repeat the words of Jesus but do not live them, we are building our lives on a sandy foundation.

God is calling you to new heights. He longs for you to be all that you can be for his kingdom. He also knows that along the way you will face trials and temptations, and if you are merely hearing the Word and not putting it into practice, you are destined for a terrible wipeout.

Jesus flat-out tells us that if we will take the time to build on his rock-solid foundation, we will not fall. No matter what may be thrown at us, we can know for certain that we will still be standing on the other side of the storm. Of course, the other option is a guarantee as well. So the choice is yours—will you stand or will you fall with a great crash?

FINDING YOUR FOUNDATION

You are getting ready to head on a mission trip. You'll probably be in a place you have never been before, meeting new people and experiencing new things. It would be really easy for you to simply say the right things and pretend to be someone you are not. Those around you may never know the truth.

However, you are called to be so much more. God has opened doors for you to go on this trip. He is calling you to grow in your faith, to become someone better than you are right now. He is opening your eyes to live differently than ever before. The challenge for you will be not just to *know* the right things to do but to put them into practice. And to do this, not just on your upcoming trip, but from now on.

By putting God's truths into practice, you are building on a foundation that is bigger than you, stronger than you, and will last for all eternity. When storms come, when challenges arise, you will have a strong launching point to make it through. It will not be empty words that you don't actually live by—it will be the eternal truth of God taking root in your heart. People will see a difference, you will experience joy, and you will take another step toward becoming the disciple of God that you are meant to be.

What kind of storms have you faced in your life? What did they reveal about your foundation?

Take some time to pray about God's plans for you on the trip to come and for your daily life. Ask him to help you put into practice the things he is teaching you. Pray that God will give you the strength to build a foundation based upon him rather than your own ideas.

My Anticipation

SUBMISSION TO GO[D]

by John Mouton

It is one of the dirtiest words in the English language. It has been known to offend, incite, and anger. People avoid it (and what it stands for) like the plague. The word is *submit*.

NEGATIVE RESPONSE

Several years ago we had a young lady (I'll call her Amy) apply to go on a mission trip with our organization, Christ in Youth. As part of the application process, Amy was required to supply us with references.

On the form that her references filled out was question #7, labeled: "Response to Authority." The choices ranged from "Openly

Rebellious" to "Submissive." One of Amy's references came back with question #7 unanswered. Instead, the responder wrote the following note: "Question #7: Amy takes direction well, if it is appropriate. She can think and make decisions independently, IF called for. Your term *submissive* is misleading and inappropriate for a functional, capable individual." The word *IF* was actually underlined twice.

Unfortunately, that man's response to the idea of submission is not uncommon. However, submission is not a dirty word to God. James tells us that we are to submit to God (James 4:7-10). The writer of Hebrews says we must submit to our church leaders (Hebrews 13:17). Paul tells us to submit to governing authorities (Romans 13:1-5). Wives are to submit to their husbands, and we are to submit to one another (Ephesians 5:21-30).

AUTHORITY PROBLEM?

If someone filled out an evaluation form for you right now, how would they rank you on question #7, "Response to Authority"?

A short-term mission trip is a great context in which to evaluate your submission to Christ as Lord. There may be things you will be asked to do, places you will be asked to go, or things you will be asked to eat that will put you far outside your comfort zone. Sometimes I think that we as Christians find ourselves saying, "I would do *anything* for God, but . . ."

Peter was struggling with this very issue when God told him in a vision to do something. Peter replied, "Surely not, Lord!" (Acts 10:14). It was after God showed Peter the importance of submission that Peter wrote: "I'm sure you have heard about the Good News for the people of Israel—that there is peace with God through Jesus Christ, who is Lord of all" (Acts 10:36, *NLT*).

If God gave you a vision like Peter's, what would he lower in your sheet? In other words, what task does God have in store for you that you are unwilling to perform right now?

INCOMPARABLE GIFTS

Having a humble and submissive heart is a daily choice we make. The blessings and peace we gain from surrendering ourselves to God are incomparable gifts of grace.

Pray that God will help you be more like Jesus, who showed us how to submit. Pray that when you face challenges and difficulties you will be able to say, as Jesus said, "Not as I will, but as you will" (Matthew 26:39). Pray that as you go on your mission trip you will serve humbly, submitting to God and those he has put in authority over you.

My Anticipation

My Anticipation

BE STRONG IN THE LORD

by Lindsey Miller

Does your upcoming mission trip seem like a daunting task? Then you might relate to Joshua. Joshua's story is one of my favorites in the Bible. In Joshua 1 we read that Moses had just died and the Lord called Joshua up to take Moses' place.

Let's put that last sentence into perspective. Moses was the one who led the Israelite people out of slavery in Egypt. Moses was involved in the great sea split, when the people escaped through the Red Sea on dry ground. Moses received the Ten Commandments from God. Moses saw the back of God! Check out what Deuteronomy says about Moses in Deuteronomy 34:10-12: "Since then, no prophet has risen in Israel like Moses, whom the LORD knew face to face, who did all those miraculous signs and wonders the LORD sent him to do in Egypt—to Pharaoh and to all his officials and to his whole land. For no one has ever shown the mighty power or performed the awesome deeds that Moses did in the sight of all Israel."

That's quite a compliment! Moses has some big sandals to fill! Now granted, Moses was not perfect. But if I were Joshua, I would be just a little bit intimidated to take on the leadership after him!

YOU WANT ME TO DO *WHAT*?

Just for kicks, see how God responds to Joshua's intimidating new responsibility. Read the entire first chapter of Joshua and make a little tally mark each time you read the words *be strong*. I counted four times, and that does not include the times God told Joshua that he would never leave or forsake him! Joshua is getting ready to fight some pretty big battles, and I can't help but wonder if Joshua was thinking, *Lord, are you kidding? You want me to do* WHAT?

You want me to do WHAT? I have that same thought every time I read Scripture and God tells me to deny myself, take up my cross, and follow him. I also think this every time I read that I am supposed to put others before myself. I think this when I realize how incredibly weak and sinful I am compared to a holy, all-powerful God. I think this when I see what God has put before me but discover that I have been distracted by the lies that the enemy put in my path.

WHAT DOES THAT MEAN?

Now go back to Joshua. God gave Joshua an enormous task, but he did not leave Joshua alone to complete it. God told Joshua to be strong and courageous because God would be with him. What a powerful thought! But what does that mean? What does it mean to be strong in the Lord? Reread Joshua 1:6-9. The answer: being strong in the Lord is being completely grounded in his truth.

Paul encourages the same thing in one of his letters. He says: "Be strong in the Lord and in his mighty power. Put on the full armor of God so that you can take your stand against the devil's schemes" (Ephesians 6:10, 11). Paul then proceeds to provide a dress code of sorts to help us visualize what being strong in the Lord looks like. Read Ephesians 6:10-18.

DRESSED FOR SUCCESS

First, Paul says to have "the belt of truth buckled around your waist." We all know that belts are great things because they hold everything in place. (Some of you may need to look into the idea of getting a belt!) What a great visual Paul provides. Truth needs to be buckled around our waists, holding everything in place.

Second, keep "the breastplate of righteousness in place." The breastplate protects the vital organs, such as the heart and the lungs. I love this picture—righteousness, God making you and me right and acceptable in his presence. This is our spiritual breastplate, protecting us against the accusations of the devil.

Next, we wear shoes that are "the readiness that comes from the gospel of peace." And we're to hold on to the shield of faith—when we believe in the power of God, we can extinguish the lies that Satan tries to throw at us.

Paul then says to take the helmet of salvation, along with "the sword of the Spirit, which is the Word of God." As the helmet protects the head, salvation provides life eternally. And the Word of God is a powerful weapon that we can use. Hebrews 4:12 says, "The word of God is living and active. Sharper than any double-edged sword, it penetrates even to dividing soul and spirit, joints and marrow."

God promised Joshua that if Joshua obeyed the Word and did not let it depart from his mouth, Joshua would be prosperous and successful (Joshua 1:8).

STANDING STRONG IN OUR BATTLES

When I was in the fourth grade, my favorite outfit was stirrup pants with a T-shirt tied at the waist. It is funny how quickly clothing styles change.

I can tell you one thing—when you are fitted in the armor of God, you will not have to worry about changing fashions or styles. You will be clothed in the finest attire, protected by the grace found in salvation, fighting with the powerful, transforming words in Scripture.

As we dress ourselves in the armor of God, we cover ourselves in the truth about the one who sends us into battle: our creator, sustainer of the universe; our Father, who created us for his glory and provided a way for us to be reconciled to him.

How are we strong in the Lord? By trusting in his Word and knowing that this life is but a mist—soon we will all be united with him forever. When we carry that hope with us, we can be strong in the Lord, standing against the battles of this world. We carry that hope when we, like Joshua, obey the words the Lord has given us and when we meditate on his truth, not letting it depart from our hearts and mouths.

What battles do you anticipate facing on your mission trip? How can Joshua's story give you confidence? Which piece of God's armor have you not yet put on?

Pray that God will clothe you in his strength for upcoming battles you must face.

My Anticipation

_____
_____
_____
_____
_____
_____
_____
_____
_____
_____
_____
_____
_____
_____
_____

My Anticipation

_____

_____

_____

_____

_____

_____

_____

_____

_____

_____

_____

_____

_____

_____

_____

REVERENCE

by Lori Murilla

Reverence means to regard somebody or something with deep respect. Most often we think of reverence as being directed toward God, who is worthy of all devotion and also fear. Actually, the Bible commands us to revere or respect God at all times. "Since you call on a Father who judges each man's work impartially, live your lives as strangers here in reverent fear" (1 Peter 1:17).

Reverence can come in all shapes and sizes, including reverence for other people and even reverence toward the fearful abilities of our enemy. But what does it mean to live in reverent fear of God and reverence for the mission of his kingdom? How can reverence make a difference on the mission field?

REVERE BY BEING STILL

We can show an attitude of reverence toward God through stillness and quietness.

Read Psalm 23. You can learn several ways to revere God in this famous psalm. You have a reverent heart toward God when you know he is your shepherd (v. 1), when you are content with all he has given you (v. 1), when you know it is he who brings you peace (v. 2), and when you don't fear death because you walk with God (v. 4).

We lead busy lives, don't we? David, the writer of Psalm 23, wrote of the blessing that comes when we lead lives in the opposite way. Revering God comes from resting in his presence and honoring who he is (Psalm 37:7). In order to enjoy the blessings that come from rest, the effort needed on your part is simple—resting.

Prepare now to maintain a reverent attitude on your mission trip by being still. There may be moments when you'll have to spend time waiting. Perhaps at the airport—as you're leaving on your adventure or arriving at your destination—something will happen that forces your group to WAIT. It may be tempting to get frustrated and agitated. In those circumstances, remember the still and quiet reverence found in Psalm 23 and recognize that God is in control.

Did you ever stop to think that you may be living life too fast and this particular mission trip experience is a blessed way for your soul to catch up?

Are waiting, being still, and resting struggles for you? Consider things you might try to participate in some quiet reverence toward God this week.

REVERE BY LISTENING TO INSTRUCTION

Another attitude of reverence is by listening to spiritual instruction.

Read Luke 10:39 about Mary's reverence toward Jesus: "Her sister, Mary, sat at the Lord's feet, listening to what he taught" (*NLT*). Mary caught the concept of reverence. In order to grow in spiritual wisdom and understanding, she positioned herself lower than her spiritual instructor.

In order to develop a strong sense of spiritual maturity, you must learn to listen. In order to listen and accept instruction, your attitude needs to be humble enough to accept a lower position than the position of those in authority over you. Have reverence for them—despite their human flaws. In order to benefit from the insight that comes from listening to spiritual instruction, the effort needed on your part is simple—listening.

Now, think about how well you accept spiritual instruction. What listening position do you have toward your leaders? Do you have an attitude of sitting at their feet in respect?

On your mission trip, you will be under someone else's instruction—the trip leader, the local church leaders, or a team member with seniority and experience. What will it take for you to lower yourself and listen attentively to another person's wisdom and spiritual instruction? You will gain important insight if you humble yourself and remain willing to listen.

REVERE BY PRAYING

Spend some time now expressing your reverence toward God. You may do so in words or in stillness. You may do so by listening and learning or by thanking God for the many ways he has given you spiritual instruction.

Talk to God about your commitment to revere him on your mission trip. Confess the times you struggle to be still or struggle to listen to instruction. Seek his help in growing in both areas. Then prepare your heart for times on your trip when you will be still and wait and times when you will sit at someone's feet and listen.

My Anticipation

_____

_____

_____

_____

_____

_____

_____

_____

_____

_____

_____

_____

_____

_____

_____

My Anticipation

THE GOD OF PEACE

by Greg Hafer

We need all kinds of peace. Peace within ourselves. Peace in our family relationships. Peace in our relationships with other people. Peace between nations. But the most important peace is peace with God. In fact, meaningful, lasting peace of any kind will depend on being truly at peace with God. Before you go on your mission trip, consider whether you are at peace with God.

SWEETEN UP!

The good news for us is that God is often called "the God of peace" (Romans 15:33; Romans 16:20; 1 Thessalonians 5:23;

Hebrews 13:20). God is interested in bringing peace into our lives.

Philippians 4:4-9 is a brief passage, but it's packed full of great ideas about how to experience "the peace of God." If you can, read the passage several times before you continue.

God wants us to be people who rejoice (v. 4). He wants us to be balanced. The "gentleness" (v. 5) that he wants to be known to all people means a "sweet reasonableness." That kind of disposition comes from being at peace with yourself, with others, and with God. Are you inclined to be sweet or sour? This passage tells us three ways to sweeten up and be at peace.

EXCHANGE WORRY FOR PRAYER

Look again at verses 6 and 7. We are told to talk to God. We get to let him know the desires of our hearts (petitions and requests) and to offer thanksgiving to him. This is an opportunity similar to the invitation of 1 Peter 5:7 that says, "Cast all your anxiety on him because he cares for you."

One word of caution: It's easy to rattle off all our requests and forget about giving God thanks. When we offer thanksgiving and realize how much God has done for us, it changes our perspective and even changes the things we really want to ask of God. If that sounds out of the ordinary, it's because it is the peace of God at work in us. His peace, which transcends all understanding, protects our hearts and minds in Christ Jesus from ordinary human understanding that would typically be filled with worry and anxiety.

EXCHANGE BAD THOUGHT PATTERNS FOR GOOD

God wants to eliminate any destructive thought process that hinders our peace. In verse 8 we find an eight-point checklist for making sure every thought is constructive:

1. Is it true? How does our thought stack up in terms of reality and accuracy?

2. Is it noble? Does the thought command respect, or is it of lesser value?

3. Is it right? Rightness should be measured to make sure our thought is on a good path.

4. Is it pure? Or is our thought defiled and contaminated?

5. Is it lovely? Does the thought move us toward brotherly love?

6. Is it admirable? Does our thought speak well of us?

7. Is it excellent? In terms of moral soundness, is the thought something at a high level, or is it questionable?

8. Is it praiseworthy? Is the thought commendable, bringing us a good reputation?

It's very easy to see that God wants us to carefully consider the content of our thought lives so we can avoid the stuff that will tear down and concentrate on the things that will build up.

EXCHANGE THE PASSIVE FOR THE ACTIVE

It's far too common for us to be on the receiving end of lots of spiritual learning through church lessons, sermons, special events, and the life examples of Christians around us—without ever doing much of anything about it. And we wonder why we have inner turmoil or feelings of emptiness.

The apostle Paul gets right to the point: "Whatever you have learned or received or heard from me, or seen in me—put it into practice" (v. 9). "Get with it!" he says. Do something about what God is teaching you and showing you!

What did Paul say will happen as a result? "The God of peace will be with you" (v. 9).

CONSIDER YOUR PEACE

Are you ready to make a few trades? Exchange worry for prayer! Exchange destructive thoughts for constructive thoughts! Exchange passive learning for active living! Consider how you can become more aware of the presence of the God of peace.

Write down some areas of your life about which you feel anxious. Ask God to allow you to experience his peace at a greater level. Then write out as many things as you can think of that you are grateful for, and tell God thanks. See if this doesn't bring a special sense of peace to your heart and mind.

Can you identify at least five things that occupy your mind on a fairly regular basis? Write them down, and then consider each one of them in light of the eight-point checklist. This will require some brutal honesty.

Think about all the spiritual learning you have had in your lifetime. What lessons do you still need to put into practice? How can you act upon the things God has taught you?

FIND ULTIMATE PEACE

My prayer for you is found in Hebrews 13:20, 21: "May the God of peace, who through the blood of the eternal covenant brought back from the dead our Lord Jesus, that great Shepherd of the sheep, equip you with everything good for doing his will, and may he work in us what is pleasing to him, through Jesus Christ, to whom be glory for ever and ever. Amen." Will you pray that prayer to the God of peace for yourself?

God brought about the ultimate act of peace through Jesus. Our sin separates us from God, making us his enemies. But because Jesus' death covered our sins, we can have peace with God and live in his presence. Praise him for bringing us ultimate, eternal peace.

God also wants you to find the peace that comes from allowing him to prepare you and use you to do his will. And certainly his will includes sharing that peace with others for whom Jesus also died. Prepare your heart now for the ways God will use you to spread his peace on your mission trip.

My Anticipation

My Anticipation

DRIVEN TO SERVE

by Bill Baumgardner

When it comes down to it, why do I serve? Several times I have asked myself that question. Do I serve because it makes me look good? It's nice to be noticed and have people look up to you because you help others. Do I serve because I feel guilty if I don't? One person told me that it was God's Spirit inside of me compelling me to serve.

So why do I serve? Because of one simple reason—Christ's example. While on earth, Jesus was the model of service. No matter where he traveled, and no matter what he was doing, he showed us what a servant was to be. Without a doubt, Jesus walked this earth as a servant.

A LIVING EXAMPLE

It was a gross job, but somebody had to do it. Usually it was left up to the lowest of servants. Foot cleaning! As you probably know, in Jesus' day, they didn't have closed shoes like you and I wear. People wore sandals—open sandals, so the grimy, dirty roads of Israel would be all over their feet. It wasn't an award-winning job to clean the feet of others.

Yet that is where we see Jesus in John 13:1-17. He placed a towel around his waist and lowered himself to serve. He served the very men who should have been serving him! In doing this, Jesus set the greatest example of service—well, the greatest before he offered his very life for us.

Did you catch it? The King of kings, our Savior, Jesus Christ, bent down to show his disciples and us that no one is above another in service. Jesus was driven to serve.

PEOPLE DON'T UNDERSTAND

People don't understand servanthood. Each summer as I organize and lead service projects, I'm consistently asked the same question: Why? Why do students give up their time, money, and effort for people they don't even know? Even though I try to explain it, people just don't get it. You know, the people in Jesus' day didn't get him either. Maybe we are in good company!

What about you? Are you driven to serve, or do you think service is beneath you? Even though you are set to go on a mission trip, your actions in the little ways show your true heart.

When you're asked to clean out the van after the trip, will you try to get someone else to do it? How about when you're asked to clean a bathroom—and that means the toilet too? Are you willing to show the love of Christ by honoring even the strange people you will meet?

Jesus' actions tell us that no job is beneath anyone and that no individual should consider himself above serving others. We have no excuses because he has already shown us that a truly driven person truly serves.

Spend some time thinking and praying about your upcoming mission trip. Confess to God any changes you need to make in your attitude in order to be a more willing servant—in the little *and* big ways. Thank Jesus for his example of service.

My Anticipation

_____

_____

_____

_____

_____

_____

_____

_____

_____

_____

_____

_____

_____

_____

_____

_____

_____

My Anticipation

_____

_____

_____

_____

_____

_____

_____

_____

_____

_____

_____

_____

_____

_____

FREE GIFTS

by Amy Sackett

Imagine being one of the twelve disciples—handpicked by God himself, studying under Jesus, and then being told to go and do what he does! How amazing is that? These misfit guys from all different backgrounds were trusted and even commissioned to go and declare that "the kingdom of heaven is near" (Matthew 4:17).

Is this really so different from you? You are part of a group (maybe you're misfits!) handpicked by God for his mission. And he is not sending you on this mission trip without power or authority. Read John 16:15. Jesus tells us that when God sends us,

his Spirit is with us so we won't be alone.
How amazing!

Perhaps comparing yourself to the disciples
is reassuring. Perhaps it's comforting to know
that God will be with you. But you still may
wonder exactly how you are supposed to go
out on the mission field and represent Jesus
to others.

FREELY RECEIVING AND GIVING

I'm sure the disciples had the same
insecurities when Jesus sent them out on
a mission. Read Matthew 10 to see Jesus'
instructions to them.

Note that Jesus said, "Freely you have
received, freely give" (v. 8). Freely they had
received what? Reading this verse in context
shows us that Jesus "called his twelve disciples
to him and gave them authority to drive
out evil spirits and to heal every disease

and sickness" (v. 1). He also gave them the power to "raise the dead, cleanse those who have leprosy, drive out demons" (v. 8). Freely they had received power to perform the ministries of God's kingdom. Now they were to freely bless others with that power in Jesus' authority.

But Christ did not send his disciples just to heal the sick and lame or to raise the dead. He sent them to tell the news that "the kingdom of heaven is near" (v. 7).

When our medical missions team is treating the sick, we offer them relief from their illnesses. But more importantly, we offer them relief for their souls. Each person that enters our clinic leaves having heard the good news of Jesus Christ. So no matter what type of ministry you will be engaged in on your mission trip—children's ministry, construction, medical missions, etc.—don't forget the most

important and lasting part of the message:
the good news of Jesus Christ.

BLESSING OTHERS AS YOU'RE BLESSED

My favorite theme of the Bible is that
people are blessed in order that they will
become blessings to others. It runs from
Genesis to Revelation. There are so many
ways in which we have been blessed and can
pass those blessings along to others. But I
can guarantee that there is no greater blessing
than that of knowing Christ and the power
of his resurrection. Now *that* is a blessing that
needs to be passed along!

God created all people with gifts. The
word *gifts* in this context means the abilities
people have that allow them to minister and
share God's blessings with others. "Each one
should use whatever gift he has received to
serve others, faithfully administering God's
grace in its various forms" (1 Peter 4:10).

Often, God gives people more than one gift. The appropriate Christian response to God's generous gifts is gratitude and thanksgiving and a readiness to share those gifts. Remember Jesus' instructions to his disciples: "Freely you have received, freely give" (Matthew 10:8). We must do the same.

It is not significant how many gifts God gives each of us; rather, it is what we do with them. One person is not greater or more important than another, even though one may have more gifts. It is not how much talent or skill or ability one has, but how one uses it.

The more gifts you have, the more responsibility God has for you. "From everyone who has been given much, much will be demanded; and from the one who has been entrusted with much, much more will be asked" (Luke 12:48).

EVALUATING YOUR GIFTS

What gifts do you think the Holy Spirit has given you? What have those gifts done for others? for yourself? Take a moment to think about the people closest to you. How has God gifted them with something that builds other people up?

Pray that God will give you boldness as you use your gifts on your mission trip to proclaim the good news about his Son. Thank him for giving you the power to speak in his name, and thank him that he is always with you—even to the ends of the earth. Pray for wisdom to know how to use the free gifts he has given you to bless those around you.

My Anticipation

My Anticipation

MASTER PLAN

by Mike Schrage

God is a nation-loving, continent-connecting, tribal-touching God! He is the mighty creator who is constantly involved in restoring his creation, and he is doing it through a master plan.

From the beginning of time, God wanted all of creation to be with him in an Eden-like experience known as Heaven. However, Satan came into the picture with an attempted coup. The tragic ramifications resulting from that war—namely sin and Hell—have infected all of us and our surroundings. The corrosiveness of sin in God's creation and the deception of sin in the hearts of people have been devastating.

On your mission trip, you may see the effects of sin more clearly than you do at home. Empty cathedrals in Europe, legalism in the religion of Islam, spiritual bondage for those under Buddhism, poverty and filth for those following Hinduism, and constant fear in the lives of people living under animism—these all indicate that sin has entered cultures, created chaos, and damaged lives.

Because of our sin, God had to come up with a salvation plan. But God's plans don't always match up with human expectation, and through the years people doubted.

PLANNING ON A NATION

The plan took shape when a new nation of people was promised to a faithful herdsman named Abram. God made a covenant with Abram (later known as Abraham) that his descendants would be created to show God's love and bless all nations and tribes (Genesis 12:1-3). But the Israelites turned their backs on God's plan and his covenant generation after generation. They turned to other gods and ignored God's blessings. Yet God continued to rescue them from their sin. He continued to forgive and show them grace. But his grace had yet to be *fully* shown.

At just the right time (meaning, God's time!), Jesus was born to fulfill God's plan, repair the covenant, and restore the relationship with descendants of Abraham and all people! Jesus came as a child, lived as a pauper, died as a criminal, and remains as a king. As long as he is king, the restoration plan is being carried out to completion.

PLANNING ON A KINGDOM

Even after Jesus died and rose again, people did not understand God's master plan. Jesus' own disciples thought God's plan was going to involve a physical kingdom rather than a spiritual one.

After Jesus' resurrection, the disciples asked if he was going to restore the kingdom back to Israel (Acts 1:6). Their hope was for dignity and self-rule out from under the oppressive hand of Rome. Christ would indeed rebuild and restore God's kingdom, but it would not be limited to Israel. And it would not be according to people's ideas or cleverness but by God's ultimate plan.

PLANNING ON SALVATION

A Pharisee named Saul heard that people were saying the man named Jesus had been God's fulfillment of the master plan. Yet Saul did not believe. Jesus did not fit Saul's plan for how God should save people.

In Acts 9, we read that Saul persecuted God's property, the church (vv. 1, 2), because he wanted nothing to do with Jesus. This persecution continued until Saul met God's plan—Jesus (vv. 3-6). The blinding meeting (vv. 7-9) was a life-altering experience.

Soon after Saul's roadside encounter with God, a Christ follower named Ananias placed his hands on Saul, and God restored sight to Saul's blind eyes—and heart (vv. 10-19). That is true restoration and complete godly renovation. Saul was now Paul—a new creation in Christ! God had a plan for Saul as a part of his ultimate plan for the world, and God used circumstances and Christians to fulfill it.

PLANNING ON REPAIR

I lived in Kenya for twenty years with my family. We had only a few conveniences in our home, and one of them was an electric mixer. One day the mixer stopped. We thought that was the end of the scrumptious cinnamon rolls, hot home-baked bread, and wonderful birthday cakes. The mixer was a special amenity in our home; without it, we would have to return to beating and whipping foods by hand or forego those treats.

I am not a technically advanced fellow, but due to necessity, I agreed to take a look at the mixer. As I opened the back and peered at the electrical wiring, I noticed a loose wire. Could it be that simple? I reattached it with little faith that something so easy could restore life, power, and spin back into our mixer. But once it was plugged in, the beaters turned! In surprise, I handed the repaired mixer back to my wife who was thrilled (as was I) with the hope of more great baked goodies to come!

Jesus was sent to repair this mixed-up, sin-laden, disconnected, nonfunctioning world that had a short with its creator.

From Abraham to the Israelites to the disciples to Saul, all people had missed God's plan. Jesus fulfilled that plan through the cross and the empty tomb. Yet God is still completing his plan for the world—his message of salvation still needs to be told to those who haven't heard. And you and I are a part of that plan.

Someday soon, Jesus will have his entire kingdom returned to his Father, and it will all be repaired, restored, renovated, and renewed. That, my friends, is good news!

If God is anything like me when I have the joy of a plan (or a machine) coming together, well . . . I cannot imagine the joy and thrill God will have to see and live with his restored creation once again, as he planned. It is all because his Son opened his life, repaired the brokenness, and renovated the relationship.

PLANNING ON A MISSION TRIP

So as you go on your journey called a mission trip, remember that you are helping complete God's plan. Look at the trip as a time to let God open up your soul, repair your spiritual wiring, and empower you to go to a waiting world filled with hurting and disconnected people from every language and culture. God is on a mission; and he would like to use you in that mission—for his enjoyment, his honor, and his glory. Are you ready to be a part of his master plan?

Take some time now to thank God for his plan to save us. Thank him for sticking with the plan through the years despite the doubts of many generations. Thank God for his redemption that he gave you in Christ. Ask the Lord to help you keep focused on his plan as you serve others on your mission trip.

My Anticipation

_____

_____

_____

_____

_____

_____

_____

_____

_____

_____

_____

_____

_____

_____

_____

My Anticipation

BROKENNESS MADE WHOLE

by Lindsey Bell

The pain came out of nowhere. Days before, I had been preparing for a cheerleading competition, practicing gymnastics, and living the normal life of a fifteen-year-old girl. But then it came.

The pain in my right foot woke me early one Wednesday morning. For the next three days, I went to three doctors and had numerous X-rays. The doctors found a fluid-filled pocket growing in the bone of my foot. The fluid continually ate away more of my bone. When I had surgery the following week, the remaining bone in my foot was only about as thick as a fingernail.

The doctors removed bone from my hip and replaced the missing bone in my foot. Six weeks later, I was able to walk again without the help of crutches.

I wish I had praised God. I wish I had looked at that trial as a chance to serve God. But I didn't. I felt cheated, scared, and angry. Looking back now, I can see how God took care of me. But I wish I had recognized his hand at the time.

One woman in the Bible who did recognize God's hand in her life is Hannah. Unlike me, she did praise God despite her pain. She's only mentioned in two chapters of the entire Bible, but her story is worth studying. Read 1 Samuel 1:1-28 and 1 Samuel 2:1-11, 18-21.

PRAISING IN BITTERNESS

Hannah didn't allow her circumstances to determine whether she approached God or not. She sought God in times of joy and in times of bitterness.

Look again at 1 Samuel 1:10, 15, and 16 to see how Hannah went to God in times of distress. Instead of getting angry or complaining about her situation, she took it before the Lord. And look what happened next: "Her face was no longer downcast" (v. 18). Because she took her troubles to God, he released her from her misery. Granted, God doesn't always release us from our miseries like he did for Hannah. Sometimes he allows us to go through difficult times and uses them to teach us and to draw us nearer to him.

Verse 19 says that Hannah and her husband Elkanah "worshiped before the Lord". Notice that God hadn't answered her prayer yet. It was only after she worshiped and after she went home that God blessed her with a child (v. 20). Nevertheless, Hannah worshiped as she waited.

What do you typically do when faced with difficulties? Take them to God or complain to a friend, get upset or angry, etc.? Or do you, like Hannah, praise the Lord even before he's answered your prayers?

HONORING GOD'S ANSWER

Hannah's dreams were eventually fulfilled. "In the course of time Hannah conceived and gave birth to a son. She named him Samuel, saying, 'Because I asked the LORD for him'" (v. 20). She remembered it was the Lord who gave her a son, and she didn't forget to praise God for her baby.

If you are anything like me, you sometimes pray, receive an answer, and then forget to come back to the Lord to thank him for it. Days may go by before I remember.

One way I remind myself is by writing down prayer requests in a journal. What steps will you take today to remember to praise God in both the joyful and hard times?

GIVING UP THE DREAM

I find Hannah's next actions amazing. She had longed for a child for years, and when she was finally blessed with one, she gave him back to God to be raised at the temple and trained as a priest (1 Samuel 1:21, 22, 24-28). I cannot imagine how difficult that must have been for Hannah. She arrived at the house of the Lord holding her precious child in her arms. She left holding nothing. She willingly gave everything she had, all of her dreams, because she knew God had given them all to her.

Yet Hannah didn't walk away from the house of the Lord upset because of her sacrifice. Instead, she rejoiced in the Lord

(1 Samuel 2:1-11). Giving back to God shouldn't be something that leaves us feeling empty; it should leave us feeling complete. And the Lord will bless us for it—maybe not in ways we'd expect, but he will bless us. Take a look at verses 18-21 to see how he blessed Hannah.

Can you think of a time when you willingly gave something back to the Lord— this could be a talent you use for his glory, money he's provided you with, etc. How did it make you feel? Have you noticed God blessing you for any sacrifices you've made? Are there things you're clinging to, hoping God doesn't ask you to give them up? If so, what are they?

BEING USED AS YOU ARE

Hannah wasn't someone most people would have thought God could use. In the culture Hannah lived in, not having children was considered a curse from God. So Hannah not only had to deal with the torment of not being able to have children, she also may have had to deal with condemning thoughts that bombarded her mind: *God has rejected me. I'm no good to him.*

But God did use Hannah to be the mother of Samuel, and Samuel became a great prophet of the Lord. God will use anyone who is willing. We tend to think God will use us only if we look a certain way, have a particular personality, or have certain talents. In high school, I thought I had to be an outgoing, vocal leader to be used by God. But God created me just the way I am—introverted and all.

Take heart. God wants to use you now—as you are, with the personality and talents he's given you. That doesn't mean we should never get out of our comfort zones. Some of the most life-changing experiences I've had occurred when I did something that seemed unnatural to me. The mission trip you are going on may feel out of your comfort zone. But God has plans to use you and your skills while you are there.

What are some qualifications you thought you had to meet in order for God to use you? How does it make you feel to know that God wants to use you just the way you are? How can that give you confidence for your mission trip?

TALKING TO GOD

Like Hannah, spend some time praising God for whatever situation you are currently in, good or bad. Evaluate your life to see if you are willing to place your dreams in God's hands and trust him to do with them what he wants.

Finally, pray for your upcoming mission trip. Let God know that you are willing to be used by him, just as he made you. Commit to trusting him to use you, even if it's outside of your comfort zone.

My Anticipation

WHATEVER

by Keith Galubski

I can remember all the different jobs I had throughout high school. I stocked shelves. I worked as a salesman. I washed dishes. I worked in a lumberyard. I worked on a truck dock. As different as all of these jobs were, they had something in common: I hated them all.

For some odd reason, each of these employers did not recognize that the world revolved around me. It was annoying. Now, I took great joy in helping around the church or helping people who went to church. I knew that when I served someone in the church, it was for God. But when it came to other areas of my life, it was about me. I failed to see all the opportunities God had placed before me to share his love with others who had never experienced it.

Paul explains in the book of Colossians how we are to view everyday life: "Whatever you do, whether in word or deed, do it all in the name of the Lord Jesus, giving thanks to God the Father through him" (Colossians 3:17). Paul's words are simple but powerful. They were intended for the people of Colosse but are still just as relevant today as they were then.

EVERYTHING YOU DO

A key word in the first part of Colossians 3:17 is *whatever*. "Whatever"— it's the answer you get when someone doesn't believe what you are telling him. "Whatever"—it's the ultimate (but lame!) comeback that's used when you cannot think of a comeback yourself.

But in this Scripture, *whatever* means something pretty powerful. *Whatever* means everything you say, everything you think, everything you plan to do or do not plan to do. *Whatever* means in everything—whether you're speaking or doing—you're supposed to do it all in the name of Jesus Christ and give him the glory.

Yikes! That hits me hard when I think about my attitude back in high school toward all of those jobs. I did not do them for God's glory.

ACCOUNTABILITY AND AUTHORITY

The second part of Colossians 3:17 holds us accountable for what we do but also gives us power and authority: "Do it all in the name of the Lord Jesus."

In Mark 9, Jesus taught his disciples about what takes place in his name: "No one

who does a miracle in my name can in the
next moment say anything bad about me, for
whoever is not against us is for us" (vv. 39, 40).

You cannot serve in the name of Jesus and
then turn around and desecrate his name.
Do not try to justify your sin or bad decisions
through the Word. God has given you the
power to glorify his name; recognize the
responsibility you have in upholding his honor.

Oftentimes, the last part of Colossians 3:17
is left out: "giving thanks to God the Father
through him." We should remember to give
thanks for every opportunity we have to serve
in God's name, because he has enabled us.

CHALLENGE

Throughout your mission trip, you will
have a schedule, a routine. First, I challenge
you to do *whatever* is set before you and to
do *whatever* is asked of you. Then I challenge

you to do it all according to Colossians 3:17. You will begin to see the meaning in picking up a piece of trash or in smiling at others. A compliment to a downcast person is like gold. Whatever you do, from this point on, do it all in the name of the Lord Jesus, and in everything you get to do, give thanks to God for that unique opportunity.

What do you do in your daily routine to take advantage of these types of "whatever" moments? What can you do on your mission trip to make sure you are aware of each "whatever" moment you have?

Confess to God the times in the past when you've acted as if life was all about you. Then make a commitment to try and live with each moment focused on God's glory, giving thanks to him. Begin today and especially keep the commitment in your heart on your mission trip.

My Anticipation

ANYONE SERVING ANYONE

by Ben Hedger

A variety of people go on mission trips each year. That variety includes people coming from different family situations, different churches, and different age groups.

Those things that make one person different from another provide an opportunity for a great life experience. You may be disappointed with your family; another person may be encouraged by his church; still another, motivated by his peers. You may have hurt someone—or been hurt. We have many experiences throughout life. And the variety of these experiences shapes who we are.

But no matter who you are, God is calling you to be part of his family and a worker in his mission field. It does not matter what you have done in the past, where you came from, or how old you are. God will use many different types of people to complete the task of sharing the gospel with all the world.

What variety of characteristics and experiences do you see in the people planning to go on your mission trip? What unique qualities do they have?

"TO SEEK AND TO SAVE WHAT WAS LOST"

God's love is amazing. He calls all people to be part of his family. Why does he do this? He does not want anyone to be lost. "The Son of Man came to seek and to save what was lost" (Luke 19:10).

Remember that God is calling you, no matter what your past or current situation.

He wants to use all people who are willing. In Mark 2:13-17, Jesus shows the magnitude of his love by eating a meal with Levi and other "sinners" and tax collectors. These were the rejected members of their community, yet they were willing to spend time with Jesus. And Jesus was willing to call them to be his followers and workers for God's kingdom.

Because you have committed to serve on a mission trip, you are already demonstrating a willingness to be like Christ. In this commitment, you must remember that you cannot have selective service. You do not get to choose whom you will and will not serve.

"WHO IS MY NEIGHBOR?"

I work with Christ in Youth. We have a service project program called Know Sweat. Many of the people whom the students serve during their week with Know Sweat are elderly or low-income families and individuals. When you arrive at your mission trip destination, you will probably make a personal assessment of people's living conditions. This is a problem if your assessment leads you to judging the individuals and questioning your commitment to serve whoever is before you.

Take a look at Luke 10:25-37. Look especially at the attitude of the teacher of the law, seen in verse 29: "He wanted to justify himself, so he asked Jesus, 'And who is my neighbor?'" Perhaps he was waiting for Jesus to tell him specifically who his neighbor was so that he could also determine which people he didn't have to bother serving at all. Yet Jesus' story didn't go the way the teacher anticipated.

In Jesus' story, the Good Samaritan showed that no matter who a person is, you must be ready to serve. You must remove social, political, and economic barriers from your mind. This will allow you to demonstrate your commitment to be like Christ.

Deep down inside, have you ever asked, "Who is my neighbor?" Think about a time when you felt God encourage you to serve, but you did nothing. Confess that situation to God. What do you need to change in order to better serve anyone God places in your path?

"FOLLOW ME"

As you serve on your mission trip, take a look at the variety of people you encounter—from those on your mission team to those you serve. Recognize how different people challenge, encourage, and motivate you—perhaps people you never expected to make a difference in your life. I hope you are encouraged by God's willingness to call anyone. And I hope you will continue to accept God's call and be motivated to serve everyone in your path.

My Anticipation

SALT OF THE EARTH

by Kacie Chase

How does it make you feel when your life is different from the lives of people around you? Alone? Scared? Proud? It can be intimidating to stand out rather than blend in. But as Christians, that is our goal.

USEFUL AND DIFFERENT

In Matthew 5:13, Jesus tells his disciples and the large crowds of people that they are "the salt of the earth." When you first read this, it may seem odd to you—why would Jesus compare people to salt? But in reality, salt has many different purposes, and it was even more important to people in the past than it is to us today.

Today we use salt for seasoning our food and for melting the ice on our roads and sidewalks. In the past salt was used as a preservative. This was very important because they didn't have freezers like we do today! The only way they had to save and store meat was to preserve it with salt. Salt also heals—like when you gargle salt water for a sore throat.

In our text Jesus tells the people to be the salt of the earth because he wanted them to be heal, preserve, and bring flavor! He didn't want them to be bland and flavorless and purposeless. He wanted them to be full of life, purposeful, and useful to the people of the world by sharing God's love with them.

In the very next verse, Jesus goes on to tell the people that they are "the light of the world." He tells them to let their light shine before others so that people may see his followers' good deeds and then praise God. Jesus wanted his people to stand out in the world. He didn't want them living the same life that everyone else was living, because everyone else was without the saving knowledge of Christ!

COMPASSION IN ACTION

"As God's chosen people, holy and dearly loved, clothe yourselves with compassion, kindness, humility, gentleness and patience" (Colossians 3:12). The Lord desires for us to be clothed with these qualities. He desires for us to be holy in his presence and live a life that is different from the lives of the nonbelievers around us. He desires for us to be salt (purposeful and useful to people) in a world that is in desperate need of it.

Read Matthew 4:23-25 and Matthew 5:1. Look how Jesus responded to the crowds of people. How does Jesus' compassion in those verses illustrate how we are to live our lives on our mission trips and in our daily lives?

Next, read Acts 3:1-10. When Peter and John reached out to the man who was disabled, look at the response from the people at the temple. Do you think that's the kind of response people would have if you went out of *your* way to help others and to be the salt of the earth?

SALTINESS IN BANGKOK

In Bangkok, Thailand, there is a group of students who display the kind of saltiness Jesus spoke of—and they do it in a way that would astound you.

In Thailand nearly every person is Buddhist, and this affects every aspect of life. When young people wake up in the morning, they are to give food or alms to the Buddhist monks, and at school they are to bow before the idols in their classrooms and say prayers throughout the day. At home their parents typically have twenty to thirty different idols or amulets sitting around.

The salty students I'm talking about live in this kind of atmosphere, yet they love Christ and serve him daily by being different from their families and friends. They tell the story of Jesus at any opportunity they get, and they refuse to pray to the idols even though their actions have gotten them sent to the principal's office and cause them to be shunned by their fellow students. Many of them even face outright rejection from their family members because of their belief in Christ.

These students are just like you and me, and they are living out their faith by letting God shape them into who he wants them to be. I can't imagine being so courageous for Christ.

ARE YOU SALTY?

Are you willing to become salty and different for the sake of the gospel? Are you willing to share Christ's love with those around you even if it scares you?

When you're on your mission trip, you may easily stand out because of where you're from in contrast to where you're serving. You may look different from the people you meet. But how can your actions set you apart as the salt of the earth? Even before you go, how can you stand out in your home community? How can you begin now to show others God's love and saving grace?

My Anticipation

My Anticipation

GOOD SOIL

by Ben Hedger

Do you ever think about where all the food in a grocery store comes from? On top of the *amount* available, you might be overwhelmed with the number of choices. For instance, do you want the name brand, organic, or locally grown kind?

As I am typing these words, oranges, lemons, and other citrus fruits we regularly eat have been damaged by unwanted freezing temperatures in areas of California. Each summer, weather conditions throughout the Midwest are discussed because of the vital role they play in a successful fall harvest. As important as these elements are to a good crop, it all begins with the quality of the soil.

When I lived in areas of farmland and livestock, I experienced the significance of dark, rich soil and the ability it has to produce lush, thick grass and large fields of corn, wheat, and soybeans. Now I live in an area that was previously mining land. A dry, thin yard surrounds my home. A couple of inches of topsoil does not compare to a couple of feet of pure, dark soil. Clearly, this is a sign that soil is very important to the growth of plants that produce the food we eat every day.

SPIRITUAL SOIL

Jesus talked about the importance of good soil in a spiritual sense. Read Matthew 13:3-9 and put yourself on the shore, looking out at the boat from which Jesus is talking. The crowd continues to move closer to the water's edge, wanting to hear clearly what Jesus is saying. He discusses the soil and its ability to respond to the seed that is thrown onto it. You may be confused and uncertain about what he says. You may wonder why this teacher and son of a craftsman is talking about farming.

Now take a look at how the disciples respond to his story and how Jesus challenges them (vv. 10-17). Jesus tells his disciples they are blessed to have received the message about the kingdom. Ultimately, the opportunity to see the Messiah and hear his words is something many over the years had desired.

Finally, read verses 18-23 where Jesus explains the parable. Jesus explains that the soil discussion he was having was truly about the growth (or lack of growth) that happens in the hearts of people who have heard the gospel.

YOU ARE THE FARMER

When you head out on your mission trip, you will be the farmer who sows the Word. As followers of Christ, you are supposed to be sharing the Bible with people who need to know who Jesus is. A recent note someone wrote me reminded me of the importance of mission trips:

A couple of people on a short-term mission trip were speaking to a group of students about American holidays. They discussed Memorial Day and Thanksgiving and then spoke of Christmas and how it is a celebration of the birth of Jesus. In response to this, a student asked, "Who is that?"

Wow! Talk about a wake-up call! There are people in the world who do not know who Jesus is. It's hard to imagine; but it's true.

SOW THE SEED

You are sowing the seed in many places, just as the parable talks about. In the explanation of the parable, Jesus talks about how each person who hears his truth will respond differently. It is important to remember that not everyone will respond the same way.

Your role of sowing is important to the growing process—1 Corinthians 3:5-9 talks of planting a seed so someone else can water it, and ultimately through God it bears fruit. Jesus says the type of soil makes a difference in how a seed will grow. Likewise, the type of person who hears the message makes a difference in how the message of God's kingdom will bear fruit. And you must understand that a person who sows does not choose whom to share the message with—everyone needs to hear!

It is then each person's choice on how to receive it. You are part of the kingdom—sow the seed.

You may be considering where God is calling you to sow the seed. In simple terms, you need to remember that everyone, everywhere needs to receive the seed. Strive to go where people have not heard about Jesus—this includes sowing seeds while you are on your mission trip and sowing seeds in your own home community.

Pray about your many opportunities to spread the Word. How do you need to prepare yourself right now to be a faithful sower of Christ's message as you go your mission trip?

My Anticipation

My Anticipation

WHEN GOD ARRIVES EARLY

by Greg Hafer

Perhaps you've heard the saying "God is always on time." That saying is so true. God is in control, and he provides for all we need—just when we need it. He always comes through, just in time.

I am becoming more and more convinced that God often arrives early in providing for our needs. In other words, he's acting on our behalf in more ways than we can imagine before we even know it. It's just that we don't always see it until later.

Can you think of some ways that God has arrived early in providing for your needs related to preparing for your mission trip?

I don't mean just the financial needs either, although that could be part of the picture. Think of people, places, events, etc., involved in your deciding to go on the mission trip.

WHILE HE WAS PRAYING

One of the ways God comes early and is actively involved in meeting our needs is through answering our prayers.

"While I was speaking and praying, confessing my sin and the sin of my people Israel and making my request to the LORD my God for his holy hill—while I was still in prayer, Gabriel, the man I had seen in the earlier vision, came to me in swift flight about the time of the evening sacrifice. He instructed me and said to me, 'Daniel, I have now come to give you insight and understanding. As soon as you began to pray, an answer was given, which I have come to tell you, for you are highly esteemed'" (Daniel 9:20-23).

Daniel had been crying out to God, pleading on behalf of Israel and the holy city, Jerusalem, because the people of God were in captivity. In this instance, a special expression of grace was given to Daniel, as the angel Gabriel was sent to him to communicate God's answer. But get this—Gabriel came with God's answer *while Daniel was still praying*! God came early! The answer was given as soon as Daniel *began* to pray. Now that's what I call powerful prayer!

DANIEL'S PRAYERS

Wouldn't it be great to see God arrive early in response to our prayers? What made the difference for Daniel? Consider some of the hints from our Scripture text, Daniel 9:20-23, and from Daniel's prayer found in Daniel 9:4-19.

- Daniel was confessing his own sin.

- Daniel was confessing the sin of his people, Israel.

- Daniel was pleading for God's mercy.

- Daniel was a pretty impressive guy, but his appeal was based on God's character, mercy, and glory, not on Daniel's (see vv.17-19).

It's almost as though God was just waiting on Daniel to begin praying so God could arrive early—as soon as Daniel started.

HINDRANCES TO PRAYER

Truth be told, most of us haven't even begun to experience God's power through prayer. There can be lots of reasons for this. Check out these Scriptures and see if any describe you:

- Trying to impress people more than talking to God (Matthew 6:5-8).

- Faithless prayers—no real confidence that God hears or that he will do anything in response (James 1:5-8).

- Simply neglecting prayer altogether (James 4:2).

- Praying with wrong motives (James 4:3).

Is it possible that God is just waiting on you to begin sincerely praying so he can arrive early?

EXPERIENCE GOD'S ANSWERS

Is there a specific issue that you need to take before God in genuine prayer? What things about your mission trip do you need to take to God in prayer? What might be getting in the way of your being able to experience the power of God through prayer?

Take time to pray right now—talk to God. No pretense, no fancy words, no self-justification, no personal agenda—just talk to God—he's waiting. Give him a chance to arrive early for you.

Take time to listen to God right now. He might want to prompt you in some way that will allow him to use you so he can arrive early for someone else. Write down any promptings you sense as you listen.

Don't be in too big a hurry as you talk with and listen to God. And when you're on your mission trip, take time to see God and experience him. He's already at work.

My Anticipation

_____
_____
_____
_____
_____
_____
_____
_____
_____
_____
_____
_____
_____
_____
_____
_____

My Anticipation

CRACKED POTS

by Wade Landers

Have you ever asked God to help you see the world the way he does? Have you ever asked God to shape you or mold you? Maybe in a moment of complete honesty, you wanted to be more Christlike. How open are you to letting God do those very things you ask of him?

WORKING THE WHEEL

It was my first trip to Taiwan, and I was blown away. I had been to other countries on short-term mission trips before. I even lived in the country of Haiti for a period of time with my wife and kids. But I had never been to a city that was so big and so crowded with people in such a small area. There are over six

149

million people living around the capital city of Taipei. It is a major metropolitan city; one of the tallest buildings in the world is located there. Most of the people who live there are not followers of God, instead choosing to worship idols, which literally number in the tens of thousands. Many Taiwanese people have never even heard the name of Jesus!

The missionaries we were working with decided to divide us into small groups—a couple of Taiwanese people with a couple of Americans. We were to spend the day together. It was an amazing experience. My favorite part was visiting an art section of the town and getting to work in an actual potter's shop.

The room was lined with shelves, all holding pots of various shapes and sizes. In the front were three potter's wheels and three stools. We got to actually throw our own lumps of clay and form them into pots that we would keep.

To make a clay pot and make it right, you have to work the clay, be willing to get a little messy, and be patient. Over and over again, the teacher helped me build the pot up and then smash it back down to work out the bubbles and flaws. It took time and hard work! But in the end, it was worth it. I had a fairly decent piece of pottery to take home as a souvenir, and I had an experience I would never forget!

GOD, THE POTTER

In Jeremiah 18:1-6, we read about a potter and God comparing himself to that potter:

"This is the word that came to Jeremiah from the LORD: 'Go down to the potter's house, and there I will give you my message.' So I went down to the potter's house, and I saw him working at the wheel. But the pot he was shaping from the clay was marred in his hands; so the potter formed it into another pot, shaping it as seemed best to him. Then the word of the LORD came to me: 'O house of Israel, can I not do with you as this potter does?' declares the LORD. 'Like clay in the hand of the potter, so are you in my hand, O house of Israel.'"

Catch the phrase "shaping it as seemed best to him." Do you believe God really knows best? Give an example from your own life of how you saw God work and how it increased your faith that he knows best. Would you describe your life as "clay in the hand of the potter"? Can God do with you what he wants?

On a short-term mission trip, there is often more opportunity to hear God because you are less distracted, less busy, and less consumed with self. Will you ask God to mold you? Will you ask him to shape you in any shape he chooses?

Reread Jeremiah 18, and think through what you want God to teach you on this trip. Then write out a prayer to God. What will you ask of him?

My Anticipation

My Anticipation

_____
_____
_____
_____
_____
_____
_____
_____
_____
_____
_____
_____
_____
_____
_____
_____
_____
_____

My Anticipation

Anticipate. Experience. Reflect.
SERVE!

For more information on how you
or your group can SERVE as
Kingdom workers through CIY's mission trips,
go to www.ciy.com/missions

CHRIST IN YOUTH

For more information on attending
CIY's High School, Jr. High, and Preteen ministry events,
go to www.ciy.com

Or contact us at:
Christ In Youth • PO Box B • Joplin, MO 64802 • 417-781-2273